God is Life

Nancy Sabato

God Is Life

Cover design & Photography by Nancy Sabato

Dedication Page

I am dedicating this book "God Is Life " to my Mother

Elizabeth DePietro Carlisle, she was a dedicated Housewife and Mother, she suffered for many years with RA and knew the difficulties she would have taking care of our family and took it all in by her unselfishness. She Loved Jesus and was a fervent prayer.
My Mother went back to her heavenly home with Jesus when she was 69 years old. She had suffered with this disease for almost 40 years.

 I dedicate this book to My Mother so that she knows that she left a legacy to her children and grandchildren with Loves, praises and glorifies the Lord through words and Prayer. She was proof that anything is possible with God; though it may be a struggle it's what God wants for His people, for the generations to rise up to be a good and kind people that are blessed and can bless others.

So I say to all the Mothers out there, you have been blessed by God with the children you have, it's up to you to love and teach them goodness, kindness and respect for God and others, to obey His commandments while praising and worshipping His Only Son Jesus Christ the Lord, Through Him all things are possible.

John 3:16

God so loved the world that He gave His one and ONLY Son, so who ever shall believe in Him shall never perish but have **everlasting life***.*

Introduction- God Is Life

This book is written for all those who are seeking to understand what Jesus did for us on the Cross-, Our Father God in Heaven gave Him up for us. Through the prophet Isaiah we see that Jesus was foretold many hundreds of years before He was born of a Virgin, (Mary) became a teacher, healer and then redeemer for us all. When you first seek God you do not realize the depth of the word of God in your life.

God is breath, life, water, blood and spirit and when Jesus was crucified for us all the sins that you can have ever committed have been washed away when you come to Jesus in repentance asking for forgiveness of your sins thus welcoming you into everlasting life with God.

If you are holding onto bitterness because someone has hurt you, God will see this as a judgment, as the scriptures say, "judge not, or you will be judged", instead why not grow your life with God by humbleness, seek Him and know, all the things that Christ has done for us and that's exactly when the heart begins to heal.

My relationship with Christ is always growing, stronger and deeper as he teaches me to be more like Him, taking more from my worldly life and picking up my cross, as he taught his disciples to do, to carry on in this world in the Name of Jesus and to spread his word to all the Nations. That is our job requirement when you follow Him, to have Godly ambition.

Table of Contents

Chapter 1

Foretold

Before Christ giving Himself up for us, the Jewish people would sacrifice an animal as their sin offering, when Jesus came, He did this for us as a human sacrifice as foretold in Isaiah, do you see the connection? He gave Himself up for us, as a human sacrifice so we never have to sacrifice the animals again. His blood was a testimony of love and forgiveness.

He did this just for us!

Isaiah was a Prophet of God and can be found in the Old Testament, He spoke to the people of Judah and foretold the coming of the Messiah in the future, just before the end of His life on earth. This was written somewhere around 681 BC

As you read through the chapters of Isaiah, look at the connection to how God placed this prophecy in the mind of Isaiah.

Isaiah 53:1

Who has believed what we have heard?
And to whom has the arm of the Lord been revealed?

Like today, the people of Jesus time were skeptics, laws were in place but their hard hearts and their worldly possessions would consume them, instead of believing in Gods gift to the world through a child but they believed in the world instead, turning their backs on truth. The Pharisees and Sadducees said it wasn't Jesus, but little did they realize they were denying the one and only Son of God

God reveals to us that we will see the promise, the coming of Jesus on the last day.

Isaiah 53:2

For he grew up before him like a young plant, and like a root out of dry ground; he had no form or majesty that we should look at him, nothing in his appearance that we should desire him.

Jesus Our Lord, born in a stable, living a humble, quiet life, not of royalty but lived among people and was not visible yet as the King so that His time on earth would be looked upon as one who is a servant.

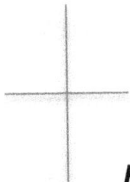

Isaiah 53:3
He was despised and rejected by others, a man of suffering and acquainted with infirmity; and as one from whom others hide their faces he was despised, and we held him of no account.

Jesus own people rejected Him, the Priests despised him and Pharisees, whose ears were covered by their own sins, rejected His message of the truth.

Isaiah 53:4-5

Surely he has borne our infirmities and carried our diseases; yet we accounted him stricken, struck down by God, and afflicted.

But he was wounded for our transgressions, crushed for our iniquities; upon him was the punishment that made us whole, and by his bruises we are healed.

Jesus was beaten, whipped beyond recognition, he was mocked, sworn at, nailed to a cross and left to die because He loved us, He took the sins of the world and nailed them to the cross.

Our life He protected and as our redeemer and set us free. Through His agony and pain we are healed and His forgiveness abounds, His life a testimony to us.

This is what Jesus did for us:

Luke   23:4-5 Then Pilate announced to the chief priests and the crowd, "I find no basis for a charge against this man" But they insisted, "He stirs up the people all over Judea by his teaching. He started in Galilee and come all the way here"

Jesus was taken away by soldiers, accused of treason, rebellion and without committing any crime, the people turned away, yet he kept quiet, knowing full well why he was there.

Think about this, can you imagine how he felt as the very own people that He loved and spoke with deserted him? Even Peter a servant of Christ turned his back on Jesus, but he forgave Him, like he forgives us.

He cared for us more than Himself, becoming a holy sacrifice.

Isaiah 53:6-7
All we like sheep have gone astray;   we have all turned to our own way, and the Lord has laid on him the iniquity of us all.
He was oppressed, and he was afflicted, yet he did not open his mouth; like a lamb that is led to the slaughter, and like a sheep that before its shearers is silent, so he did not open his mouth

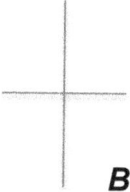

Isaiah 53:8

By a perversion of justice he was taken away. Who could have imagined his future? For he was cut off from the land of the living, stricken for the transgression of my people.

Could you imagine going to the cross for others, for sins of the entire world, he bore that shame?

Jesus did this to show is deep love for us, taking the cross, carrying the burden, as we turned away, He carried us. His life was a testimony for all; do we become more like, the world or Jesus?

As we become more like Jesus we give up our selfishness, wrong living, we give up our lives to grow in Him and serve the people in this world, gratifying our souls and not self.

God is Life & in All Things

Isaiah 53:10-11-12

Yet it was the will of the Lord to crush him with pain. When you make his life an offering for sin, he shall see his offspring, and shall prolong his days; through him the will of the Lord shall prosper. Out of his anguish he shall see light; he shall find satisfaction through his knowledge. the righteous one, my servant, shall make many righteous, and he shall bear their iniquities. Therefore I will allot him a portion with the great, and he shall divide the spoil with the strong; because he poured out himself to death, and was numbered with the transgressors; yet he bore the sin of many and made intercession for the transgressors.

Jesus gave himself up on the Cross, Isaiah foretells this, like a lamb to the slaughter", God's ultimate sacrifice -His one and only Son. Jesus took the cross, a servant call from His Father in heaven, the Father giving us His only Son so we may have life everlasting in heaven with Jesus, what a great triumph over death, covering us with His love this way, just for this world!

John 10:14-18

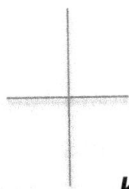

"I am the good shepherd; I know my own sheep, and they know me, just as my Father knows me and I know the Father. So I sacrifice my life for the sheep. 16 I have other sheep, too, that are not in this sheepfold. I must bring them also. They will listen to my voice, and there will be one flock with one shepherd.

"The Father loves me because I sacrifice my life so I may take it back again. No one can take my life from me. I sacrifice it voluntarily. For I have the authority to lay it down when I want to and also to take it up again. For this is what my Father has commanded.

God the Father had a plan when Adam and Eve sinned, God provided a part of His own self, His one and only Son to come in and to be a Holy sacrifice for His people, no longer did they need an animal, Jesus was the sacrifice, one sacrifice, fully man and fully God, for you and me so that our sins can be forgiven.

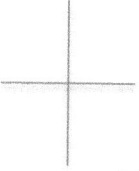

Isaiah 53:9

They made his grave with the wicked and his tomb with the rich, although he had done no violence, and there was no deceit in his mouth.

Jesus was given His sentence with the criminals; He had no tomb but was given one by Joseph of Arimathea (a secret disciple)
He never blamed anyone nor did He accuse for putting this crime on Him and knew His fate. He loved us all, even the ones who put Him on the cross.

Maybe somewhere in your life you have done wrong, but you must remember that God never turns away from you, God loves you and gave Jesus to us as a gift showing us His loving sacrifice.

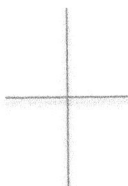

Reflection On Jesus

Galatians 5:24

Paul writes:
Those who belong to Christ Jesus have crucified the flesh with its passions and desires

When you follow the world, you strive to do things that the world thinks are great and that is ok, but it's not lasting.
God wants us to strive to be better, but are you striving to be better for the world or for God? For the things on earth that won't last or for a future home in Heaven?

This world is temporary but the things of God are eternal.
Some people live for the pleasures of today, but what would happen if you lost it all? What If you lost your stuff or your health wasn't right and you were not recovering as quickly, but you had your material things, do you think that this will sustain you? But a relationship with God is eternal, forever with Him in Heaven, better than what you will leave on the earth when you die.. The things of God are to be put first, not second. When you let go of the worldly things of this life and let God work in your life the way He needs to, then you can be set free from the sin and burden because He did this for you at the cross.

So reflect on Gods eternal ways not the ways of this earthly life but your eternal life ahead with Jesus in Heaven.

Psalm 62:1 My soul finds rest in God alone: my salvation comes from Him.

The Water, The Spirit, The Blood

> *1 John 5:6-8*
> *John says:*

> *This is the one who came by water and blood-Jesus Christ. He did not come by water only, but by water and blood. And it is the Spirit that testifies, because the Spirit is truth. For there are three that testify - the Spirit, the Water and the Blood and the three are in agreement*

Through the power of the Blood of Christ, our sins are covered and we are in holiness by the eternal word of God through the scriptures and gospels, we have been redeemed. He gave us the Holy Spirit to be with us as our life guide, pray for the Holy Spirit to guide you.

Jesus is Living water that flows

Chapter 2

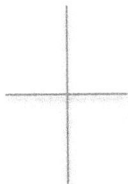

Jesus Is Our Redeemer

Isaiah 59:20

"The Redeemer will come to Jerusalem to buy back those in Israel who have turned from their sins," says the Lord.

Jesus came into the world for us, giving himself up.

Matthew 27:50-54

And when Jesus had cried out again in a loud voice, he gave up his spirit.
At that moment the curtain of the temple was torn in two from top to bottom. The earth shook, the rocks split and the tombs broke open. The bodies of many holy people who had died were raised to life. They came out of the tombs after Jesus' resurrection and went into the holy city and appeared to many people. When the centurion and those with him who were guarding Jesus saw the earthquake and all that had happened, they were terrified, and exclaimed, "Surely he was the Son of God!"

Before Jesus died on the cross at 3:00pm he cried out to His Father saying, "into your hands I commend my spirit, it Is finished", and God took Him. Suddenly an earthquake, the sun was darkened, the curtain that separated the Holy of Holies in the temple was torn in half from top to bottom signifying that there was no longer separation from God because of what Jesus did on the cross.

But it's not over! It's triumphant!
Jesus defeats death and is resurrected.

1 John 5:1-2

John tells us:
Everyone who believes that Jesus Christ is born of God and everyone who loves the Father loves His child as well. This is how we know we are the children of God: by loving God and carrying out His commands.

If you have not given your life over to Jesus do it now. He is waiting for you and wants you to pray for your needs. There is always love waiting for you, the Father in Heaven loves you more than you could possibly understand. Count your blessings, count them in all the ways you can, thank your Father in heaven for it all.

Psalm 24:4 Show me your ways. O Lordt each me your paths.

Do you want a relationship with Jesus and have him come into your life? Pray this prayer:

Lord, Jesus, please come into my life and forgive me of my sins. I want a relationship with you, please save me from this world and it's temptation of sin, I want to make you my Lord and Savior so that I may live with you eternally in the Heavenly Kingdom someday.
Amen

Love For God

1 John 5:3-5

> *John writes:*

This is love for God:

To obey His commands, and His commands are not burdensome. For everyone born of God overcomes the world. This is the victory that overcomes the world, even our faith. Who is it that overcomes the world?

Only He who believes that Jesus is the Son of God

Believe in Jesus and you will be saved, for we are citizens of heaven and the earth is fading away. What a privilege to know Jesus, do you know how blessed you are because you can have a relationship with Jesus and the Spirit of God can live in you?

Do you know that you were born just at this time to reflect Jesus in the world?

What a privilege to know Jesus, you were born for this!

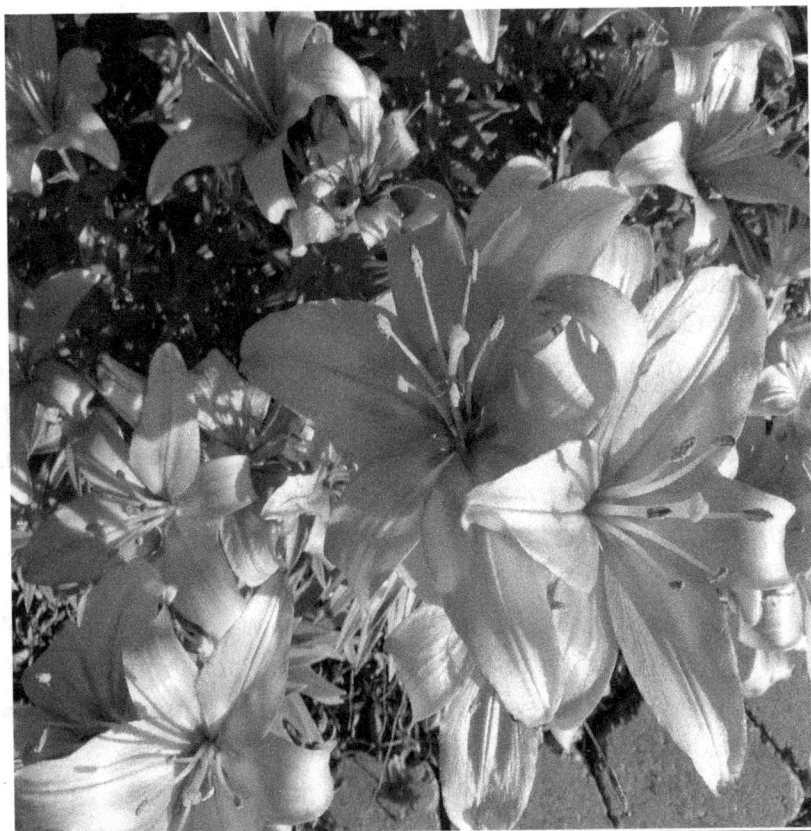

Psalm 63:4 I will praise you as long as I live and in your name I will lift up my hands.

The Promise Of the Holy Spirit

Isaiah 59:21

"And this is my covenant with them," says the Lord. "My Spirit will not leave them, and neither will these words I have given you. They will be on your lips and on the lips of your children and your children's children forever. I, the Lord, have spoken.

In the Book of Acts, chapter 2, the disciples were waiting for the promise of the Holy Spirit *"suddenly the sound a violent wind came from heaven" Acts 2:2* -when it came it was a rushing wind, with the capacity of allowing breath and life into those whom God has chosen to speak for Him. You are a child of God, whom He loves and desires to give you the Holy Spirit to live in you.

John 14:15 -18

John 14:15-18 Jesus says:

If you love me you will obey what I command, and I will ask the Father and He will give you another Counselor to be with you forever- the Spirit of truth.
The World cannot accept Him because it neither sees him or knows him but you know Him He lives with you and will be in you. I will not leave you as orphans I will come to you.

Jesus promised the disciples, he would give us the Holy Spirit and those who follow Him, know they will never be alone, that whoever comes to Christ will inherit the free gift of the Holy Spirit as a guide for our life as protection from the evil one that lives in this world. The Holy Spirit will bring light to your dark moments and live within you so you may reflect Jesus to others.

Born Again

John 3:6-8

> *Jesus says:*
> *I tell you the truth, no one can enter the kingdom of God unless he is born of water and the Spirit. Flesh gives birth to flesh but the Spirit gives birth to spirit. You should not be surprised at my saying,*
> *You must be born again, to see the Kingdom of God*

Do you pray for a relationship with Him? Are you seeking the Holy Spirit in your walk with Christ, Jesus asks you to pray, pray for the counselor, the Spirit of truth, the Holy Spirit of God - through the Holy Spirit you can find your guidance in your life daily. Because Jesus tells us He will not leave us as orphans, through the Holy Spirit He works in us.

Jesus desires a relationship with you, right now, today.
Are you seeking him?

The Road before you know Christ

The road before is like this, dreary and bleak.

When the Holy Spirit comes into your life,
You are raised up with Christ and everything becomes new!

Knowing Jesus

John 8:17-18

Jesus said:

" In your own law it is written that the testimony of two men is valid. I am the one who testifies for myself: my other witness is the Father who sent me,

To know that Jesus came to give His life as a ransom for us and that God our Father gave up His only Son so that we are set free through the Water, the Spirit and the Blood.

Do you long for peace in your life? Do you feel as though God is calling you to Him? Respond through prayer and asking. He gives us direction and wants us to read the gospel given to us, it's direction for your soul.

Follow Jesus.

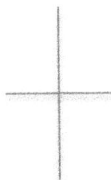

God's Testimony

1 John 5:9-12

John says:
We except man's testimony, but God's testimony is greater because it is testimony of God which He has given about His Son. Anyone who believes in the Son of God has this testimony in His heart, anyone who does not believe God has made him out to be a liar because he has not believed the testimony God has given about His Son. And this is the testimony, God has given us eternal life and this life is His Son. He who has the Son has the life, he who does not have the Son of God does not have life.

Reflect on this day and know that is it given by the Lord for you. Trust and believe that He gives the secret things of God (Deuteronomy 29:29) to those who trust and obey Him. Glorious and holy is the Lord and with all the things that we are blessed with, let us give thanks and praise everyday and glorify His name to all.

Vine and the Branches

John 15:5 -6

Jesus says:
I am the vine: you are the branches, If a man remains in me and I in Him, he will bear much fruit: apart from me you can do nothing. If anyone does not remain in me he is like a branch that is thrown away and withers, such branches are picked up, thrown into the fire and burned.

Everlasting Life through Christ

You have received life when you gave yourself to Christ, through Him you have been made whole and through Him you live and carry on the faith and the Spirit that He gives you to carry on the message of the Cross. Stand firm on the word of God, do not be swayed to this world, seek his council on all matters in your life because:

Apart from Jesus we can do nothing,

But with Jesus all things are possible

Psalm 66:1-2 Shout to God all the earth! Sing the glory of his name make his praise glorious.

First Fruits

1 Corinthians 15:22-23

Paul writes:

For as in Adam all die, so in Christ all will be made alive. But each in his own turn: Christ the first fruits, then, when he comes those who belong to Him.

Through Christ and Christ alone, your soul will be eternal in the Kingdom of God. Live for him and give the first part of your day in prayer as you ask, seek and knock.

Chapter 3

The Kingdom As An Inheritance

1 Corinthians 15:50-52

Paul writes:

I declare to you brothers that flesh and blood cannot inherit the Kingdom of God, nor does the perishable inherit the imperishable. Listen, I tell you a mystery, we will not all sleep but we will all be changed- in a flash in the twinkling of an eye, at the last trumpet.
For the trumpet will sound and the dead will be raised imperishable and we will be changed.

How will be change? The flesh decomposes but the spirit lives with Christ eternal. That is what Paul is telling us through this scripture that when we live on earth we perish but our lives with Christ are everlasting in glory and we won't die, we live and grow with Him eternally.

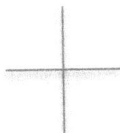

Citizenship in Heaven

Philippians 3:20-21

Paul writes:

But our Citizenship is in heaven, And we eagerly await a Savior from there, the Lord Jesus Christ, who by the power that enables Him to bring everything under His control, will transform our lowly bodies so that they will be like His glorious body.

And so, we shall be set free in Christ our Lord, when we establish our relationship with Him, we won't be interested in the things that this world offers as we live for the day when we will be with Him in eternal heaven, our real home as our earthly bodies decay and we will have our spiritual new bodies glorified by Him in the resurrection of the dead.

Heaven is our eternal home for all who believe that Jesus Christ is Lord.

Earthly Desire

Philippians 3:19-21

Paul tells us "many will live as enemies of the cross of Christ. Their enemy is destruction and their god is their stomach their glory is in their shame, their mind is set on earthly things."

If your life is full of faith in the material things of this world that perish, then what will you expect at the end of your life, since this is where you store your treasure, your passion has not been a rich relationship with God.

In the Last Days

Spoken by the Prophet Joel

Acts 2:17-18- In the last days, God says I will pour out my spirit on all people your sons and daughters will prophesy, your young men will see visions, your old men will dream dreams. Even on my servants both men and women will pour out my spirit in those days and they will prophesy.

2 Peter 3:3-4
First of all in the last days scoffers will come, scoffing and following their own evil desires, they will say where is the coming He promised?

Have you thought that God isn't coming right now? Jesus said to be ready and God knew the beginning and the end, it has been in his plan all along. God assures us through His word that the evil people of this world will fall to it on judgment day, that is when God destroys the present earth with fire. Where do you stand with God today, where will you spend eternity and do you think you will go to Heaven when you die?

As We Wait For Christ's Return

Be prepared and ready for the day Christ returns. Learn to live as he asked us to: in kindness, love and joy, committing ourselves to him in everything. When we die to our self driven lives and seek Jesus, we then became alive in Christ.

In your everyday life are you walking with the Lord through your deeds, work, and reflection? When you belong to Him you are held to a higher purpose and are accountable for your actions concerning what we do and don't do. One of the best books in the Bible New Testament is James (half brother of Jesus) James writes about how a Christian should behave as well as teaches us a faith walk, and how to we should live and behave according to the teaching of Jesus. Study the Bible and learn how God wants you to live. Through the Bible we become convicted of our sinful nature that we all have in us.

Pray for strength and help, it is your direct line to Jesus as he continues to seek a close personal relationship with you, when you do this, it will open your heart and mind to the things of God, you will truly understand what you have been missing all along.

Are You Ready?

Our inheritance is the Kingdom of God. No matter where you are in your journey remember that Jesus is the only way to the Father through his salvation. He holds the Kingdom in His hands and because you love Him you become a citizen with Him in Heaven for which He rules.

Where are you today?

Have you given your life to Jesus?

Are you ready to meet Jesus?

Your Journey

Life Journey

We don't know our journey, we follow Christ and do His will and because we love Him, we desire to become more like Him and less like the world, because the world is fading.

Jesus is alive and never fades. So follow Him, and you shall receive your inheritance that lies ahead,

Rejoice in the things of God that are seen and unseen, believe that the Lord is close by, He knows your heart and desires. God Is Life.

Final Reflection

Imitate God, Do good

3 John verse 11

Do not imitate what is evil but what is good. Anyone who does what is good is from God. Anyone who does what is evil is not from God.

Follow Jesus and do not be swayed to the world and ungodliness. Hold tight the promises of God our Father through struggles and blessing. Know that it is Christ that lifts you from all of this world's troubles and trials. Jesus although born a man was fully God. He is the Messiah, who came in humbleness and love to find His peace with us in our hearts and minds

Always seek God first in all things; do not trust the world or its ways. I encourage you not to hold grudges and to forgive. Is there someone that has hurt you?

Jesus tells us to forgive 70 times 7, have you reflected this?

Prayer for your Spirit

Holy God, thank you for your One and only Son.
That gives us life and breath so that we may live free from the world's desires and we want to please you Lord in ways we do not understand, but that you will reveal to your servants each day that we live for you.

God teach us to pray all the time as each moment in your presence is a moment that reflects the love that you have for us in your Son that you gave to us, that lives in us and through us, we thank you Lord.

Thank you God for the broken and sinful people so we can lead to them to you and you can bless them with your Holy Spirit. Thank you for the work you have provided on earth. God we especially want to thank you for sending your one and only Son, Jesus Christ who we love as we rejoice and look forward to for His coming again. Amen

From the Author:

Written with the direction of the Holy Spirit in mind, the book is a reminder that we are not in charge of our lives, Jesus is.

The photographs taken are a dedication to Jesus for giving his wonderful gift of flowers, clouds and landscapes. God is always encouraging us to look at the things on earth, that his creation of beauty and because of these gifts we are able to glance on the things that God has provided for us in a unique way and given this opportunity to enjoy them. Praise God for all He gives!

If you don't have a personal relationship with the Lord I encourage you to pray for one. Gods ear is open to you.

If you think someone may be struggling, I encourage you to speak to them about God. There are so many broken people in the world that need our help on their journey to know Christ. Thank you for reading this book; I hope you share it with someone who may be searching for answers, tell them about Jesus and what He came to do and continues to do.

Nancy Sabato-
Christian Writer, Speaker & Photographer

Nancy has been following Jesus from birth, but Born Again in 2008 studies scripture and attended various Bible studies through Church and classes. Nancy spent most of her life in worldly ways but through prayer and seeking, Jesus has transformed her life in the spirit to walk with Him and desire fully to learn more about Him.
We encourage you to visit the website and blog:
www.nancysabato.com
Writer, Author, Speaker, Leader and Photographer.
Web Author on subjects of families, relationships and Jesus.
www.speakersforchrist.com
Christian News, and speakers for Christ throughout the world.
A Website for ministry and connecting Christians.

If you would like Nancy to speak to your church or organization on prayer and having a relationship with Jesus, please email or call
Email: nancy.sabato@gmail.com
Or call : 201-666-8465

www.ingramcontent.com/pod-product-compliance
Lightning Source LLC
Chambersburg PA
CBHW081638040426
42449CB00014B/3371